Hunter Johnson Presents...

I0200297

LOVE HER not fight HER

Illustrated by JeT'aime Bennett

The hate that we show

Pretty Good Thinker

My good looks paired with my pedigree, often make me prettiest in the place,

But my aim is to not be regarded, as just another pretty face.

Although my hair is long and straight, the waves of my mind run very deep,

But I'm hardly heralded as headstrong heroine; smarts are what most seldom see.

I'm thankful for my good looks, but model is not my aspiring profession,

That's why I stick strong to my studies, and I go so hard on my lesson.

Too many people of the world, only see 'pretty girl' when thinking in regard to me,

And would never guess I am a Biology major, much less, that I minor in chemistry.

They put my beauty on a pedestal, like the ones where all of the queens sit,

But fail to respect me as intellectual, although I stay at the top of the Dean's List.

If they'd only take the time to connect the dots, they could see how I perfect my grind,

And if they'd, perhaps, take the time to see, maybe they would learn to respect my mind.

Green-eyed Monster

No one paid Marie very much attention, until Johnny came along,

Then, Sadie got his head to turn, and Johnny left Marie alone.

Imagine what young Marie must feel—her very devastation,

She's lost the attention of the only guy that ever gave her conversation.

Marie examines the situation, takes a long look in the mirror,

She's trying to fight back her emotions, trying harder to conceal her tears, her,

Mind is going in overdrive—the only logic she can fester,

Is that Sadie's looks and her own perceived lack, thereof, is what has let Sadie best her.

She lets her jealousy overtake her—grabs a box cutter from her purse,

Recklessly slices Sadie's face, so Johnny will notice Marie's own beauty, first.

So, now, Sadie has been disfigured, and Marie has a record, true,

Isn't it a shame, sometimes, the things that jealousy will make us do?

Fooled by Fairy Tales

They told you to do things the "right way," and your wishes would be fulfilled,

And, of course, you believed them, because you had not truly lived.

They shielded you from the world and things they thought would mess you up,

Not knowing that their constant sheltering would make you a sitting duck.

Naïve to the things around you—foreign to what should be familiar places,

Stranger to what could bring you danger—susceptible to all the smiling faces.

Showing teeth to all that meet you, putting on shows for all those willing to watch you,

Absence of alcohol education in adolescence might turn you into a martini bopper.

Saying "yes" when, all the while, you should be saying "no,"

Positioned as prey to the predators—catching cons from all the pros.

Fair game to all of the athletes, you're being branded by all of the frats,

Learning the craft while making a name for yourself, spelled "I already hit that."

You were a little princess, primped and pressed, cultured through ballet, tap, and jazz,

Now, you're getting pimped and stressed and, always, swindled out of cash.

Your parents are to thank or blame, if that's the word you choose,

They sheltered instead of preparing you, and real life is giving you the blues.

They said, "Pretty girls don't talk ugly," instead of explaining improper linguistics,

So you're intrigued by how bad boys speak; curiosity may help make you a statistic.

The moral to whoever reads this, if you haven't figured it out, yet,

Is teach your kids what real life is, or they will, surely, live to regret.

Movie Star Status

Lisa Ann friended him on Facebook, after she, first, saw him at a party,

Rico belonged to the hosting frat, and they were known to party hardy.

She was a first-year freshman—her first time far away from the house,

He was a fifth-year senior who knew he had caught himself a "country mouse."

Professing that he liked her, Rico claimed that he had longed to meet her,

If it was okay with Lisa Ann, Rico told her he would like to see her.

She obliged Rico's request and assured that she would visit him after her test,

He said that they could celebrate her "A;" he was sure that she would do the best.

Words spoken like a gentleman let her know that he was something special,

So she said to pick her up at the dorm, at a quarter past seven.

He engaged her in conversation, while making a smoothie in the kitchen sink,

And as soon as he caught her head turned, he slipped something into her drink.

All night long, he had his way with her—sexing her and truly doing,

Any and all things that he wanted to; unbeknownst to her, he even made a movie.

From then on, she was left with shame and pain from Rico's blitz attack,

The innocence and virginity that he took from her, no one could start to give her back.

Pole Tax

It seems she has it all to outsiders; the girl is getting paid,

She started stripping at the club when her school pulled her financial aid.

Sure, she can afford to pay her way and can afford expensive leases,

But the pole is taking toll on who she is and taxing her heart to pieces.

While making money in the club, she possesses such sexual prowess and power,

Can't stand to look in mirrors, while at home; she scrubs her body in the shower.

Men touch and paw at her, and she has to make like she wants it,

But with each day that passes, she finds her reflection harder to stomach.

Alexis shakes and claps and spins, and drops it down the pole,

Kisses necks—all while in laps—and gets fondled in every hole.

She should take inventory and re-evaluate the gifts that she's been given,

Before falling deeper into traps of easy money and becomes victim to her fast living.

True Colors

Is it merely morning sickness, anticipation of what she's having,

Does anxiety have her crying—having a baby and not knowing the daddy.

Like Mounties, she always gets her man in, lipstick and rouge she's so demanding,

She is a physical threat—her legs posed in heels she can't even stand in.

A body like it was wished for from a lantern—a product of milk, gallon on gallon,

It has really done her good, molding her body into a stallion.

Her virtue had always been nurtured; her daddy gave her value in fortunes,

So, there was no excuse—nothing in time to have driven her to.

Lessons of a father, her daddy taught her; she has abandoned them,

Not seeming like the same daddy's girl, she lays with random men.

Of course, there are those with expensive habits so lavish,

But some make the cut for the status that they have.

She moved from fresh meat to a sophomore, showing signs of her maturity,

Unfortunately, she has found her position compromising, victim to her promiscuity.

Sometimes, I guess we can't blame present on the past or slick brothers,

Often, it just takes a little time to be shown people's most true colors.

So Long, Somebody

Camouflaged with makeup and killer hairdos,

She would need a search party just to find her value.

She has opinions so off-based; they are of her inadequacy,

I say her opinions are so off-based, considering she has a killer anatomy.

Until this young miss arrives, the party's never starting,

But she becomes a very important person, when the others begin departing.

She sees no harm in chosen path; she isn't out there on the block,

Instead, choosing to trade pain for gain, and sleep her way to the very top.

She came to college for education but is, steadily, losing sight,

May not be a whore, but she stayed at Holiday Inn Express, last night.

Getting better at every level, male professors hand her A's and B's,

She volunteers for extra credit work—the credit going to work done while on her knees.

Her beauty radiates itself, but her potential's inconsequential,

If it weren't for how she carries herself, her bounds would be so exponential.

For the rewards she's receiving, she's steadily being penalized,

And will keep on concealing grief until it can be no longer disguised.

Wanted to be Grown

You were dying to be grown; now, you're all on your own,

You pay your own bills—for your meals and your phone.

You never could imagine—never could have dreamed,

That the life that you were living wasn't as bad as it once seemed.

Big Mama and Daddy said when to come in,

They laid down the rules and approved of your friends.

But you thought, with contempt, that parents were strict,

With their analyzing your habits and the things that you did.

Now, you're all on your own, doing what grown folks do,

Making real-life decisions, choosing your own curfew.

And what did you do, made choices, some bad,

Like partying, too much, dressing scantily clad.

Evading the truth, you've become quite the liar,

Even strayed from the church, though you, once, sang in the choir.

And your name precedes you wherever you go,

Not as a young scholar, though; you're simply known as a hoe.

Not just in your new dwelling—the present streets that you roam,

Your lifestyle's no secret; it even made it back home.

Indiscretion and poor judgment, only you are to blame,

For your family's bowed heads, you sure have caused them much shame.

Your mama's still praying for her baby that is long gone,

And all this because you thought you wanted to be grown.

Mother May I?

Donna, now, is not herself; she used to be a wholesome hen,

But, lately, she just crows with cocks—lying with multiple men.

It seems she doesn't have enough time to fit in all of the freaky relations,

Interests come and go out of her back door; men change like buses at the station.

No matter what time of day, she makes a way to get it in,

Whether chasing love on weekdays or loose freakin' on the weekends.

Kissing for comfort—lying underneath for understanding,

Receiving what is given as true love, for her, never seems to get too demanding.

She sucks as a tradeoff for softness, spreads in exchange for time spent,

Fondles for father figure she's never known; for each boyfriend, keeps her back bent.

Through all her twisting and turning, back arching and squatting,

Donna should be mindful, that her young daughter is watching.

Awaiting Game

It seemed that the potential was there—like he could run the house like Parliament,

But he needed a little polishing; he was kind of awkward like his name was Clark Kent.

Tirelessly, he chased you, endlessly—hoped that, one day, he'd be a winner,

That you would give him a second look, at least let him take you out to dinner.

So, at long last, you obliged him, decided to take him up on his offer,

Imagine the joy he must've felt—eyes probably lit up like sparklers.

You're, steadily, playing him weak, like he's not another dog that longs to bone you,

Don't know enough to know if you give in once and it's good, he'll have you when he wants to.

The Stick Blues

Her silence is somber—her charisma displaced,

Tears roll like raindrops, while wrinkles etch her face.

Pleasure is the cause; now, displeasure is abound,

Her cheeks are dampened, but there is not a single sound.

Frequent chills rip her body, through every piece of sinew,

Each glance of the stick that, now, has begun to turn blue.

Thoughts torment her mind; concentration is so hard, it,

Is a result of an impulse—an escape from regular logic.

Now, her life flashing by her, sitting on a porcelain seat, her,

Eyes red and bloodshot, golden liquid shining, still, beneath her.

Dreams of her dorm room—how she had dreamed to decorate it,

Turn to instant nightmares, before their fruition, they have faded.

Too young to reason, she can't fathom what went wrong,

The one true love of her life, presents her, now, only with a dial tone.

She wishes that she had listened to what she used to regard as just banter,

Something like nine months is what she has to come up with some answers.

Mama, Mama Can't You See

He pays the amount that the judge ordered—nothing more and nothing less,

And asks for a receipt as proof, in addition to the recorded check.

Don't misunderstand; he's a good father, and has been all the while,

But knows that his baby's mom won't spend the money on his child.

She chooses to sponsor barbecues—decorating her house like she lives in a mansion,

Pamper herself instead of their son—providing drinks of choice for her and companions.

Meanwhile, on the other side of town, on his rare off days, he puts together new toys,

Just so he can have a chance to see smiles of joy from his baby boy.

She's the baby's mother, true, but she needs a class on loving,

Her son lives with her, fine, but her attitude needs more readjusting.

The father does his best, so his child should want for nothing,

But all that the world will see is a single mother struggling.

Even though she spends the child support, and never saves a single dime,

Making sure her hair and nails are laid—won't provide for their son a single time.

Meticulous while dressing herself, but her son has been forgotten,

She looks like she's at the top of life, and her son's down at the bottom.

Fire Burns

How did this come about, how did it all begin,

He's fooled her like he loved her, now, she's pregnant with his twins.

No thinking of the sin when he was, steadily swimming in her,

Just to make sure a baby isn't within her, she usually takes a swig of vinegar.

She was head over heels for him—return on her love's deposit she was after,

Gladly, she would bare-knuckle box Big Foot, if only he would ask her.

A sucker for love she proved, but her love never grew to an obsession,

She just couldn't get enough, of how she undressed him and sexed him.

April Showers

God-given beauty queen, so she is the one he flaunts,

He calls her "boo" and "baby girl," because she gives him what he wants.

She never could've guessed it; therefore, she could never know,

That the love he gives is shallow, and that she is just for show.

Whether she knows or not, she's ever-quiet and keeps him clean,

Beautiful, she may be, but she has low self-esteem.

She does nice things and cooks and cleans and calls him just because,

And day by day, she turns blind eyes to all the things he does.

He dogs her out, flagrantly cheats, and calls her out her name,

Anytime something goes wrong, of course, she's the one to blame.

To young April, her name, by the way, I say to learn your worth,

No one will ever love you, girl, until you love you, first.

Hold Me Down

Think of all of the time you've spent, and all that you've been through,

Then, you may start to realize, he's really not that into you.

There's no reason he hasn't taken the step to wed you, now, instead of later,

And all you do is make excuses in order to keep excusing his behavior.

Don't you think ten years is long enough to weigh decisions for life?

He could have been had a made up mind in regard to making you his wife.

Are you afraid to find someone else—to do bad by yourself and be alone?

'Cause everyone is talking behind your back about how he's stringing you along.

At what point will you not let him be a boy and hold him accountable for being grown?

'Cause please believe that there is no shame and nothing wrong with moving on.

No matter how much you are for him—how many home-cooked meals you feed him,

If he's not moving, he is a hold me down, and you don't really need him.

Push Comes to Shove

It was cute when you would play fight, but you'd notice while you were playing,

He'd get overly agitated—offended by your actions and any words that you were saying.

Often, you accepted the damsel role; you liked that his power made you feel helpless,

Slowly, the way he laughed and played, went from oh so cute to far too reckless.

You are a smart young lady, so you notice but won't acknowledge the truth,

That you, long ago, moved from playful petting, and into the realm of downright abuse.

Nothing you ever do is good enough; he degrades you saying to go on a diet,

He hits you with his balled up fists or chokes you when you will not be quiet.

You are a pretty painted picture; publicly, you seem like you adore each other,

At home, you nurse bumps and bruises; he's careful to hit the areas that your clothes cover.

You've grown to become nervous in his presence—a trembling voice anytime he's near,

Instead of shuttering from thoughts of his touch, your body gives off tremors of fear.

Please do not sell yourself short in order just to have a man to come home to,

Trust and believe that he does not love you, if he chooses to put his hands on you.

This is a simple truth, but it is more than just words,

The more you accept and enable behavior, the more you think it's what you deserve.

The Greatest Show on Earth

She would bend over backward—did all she could for the clown,

Gave him any sex he could request; like Mary J., she was always going down.

Bobby became a narcissist, living and dying by his illustrious image,

Like the circus fellows say, a new sucker is born into this world every minute.

Constant subject to a self-made monarch, she takes it in and, all the while,

Hurt is evident in her, but she still manages to muster a smile.

And although she doesn't like, it seems as though he really loves it,

The shrink in her demeanor, when he shows out on her in public.

Barking orders, the names he calls her, leave her mind stressed and in a fog,

You should see the treatment he greets her with; it's not fitting for a dog.

She has accepted his second class treatment, even when her butt gets beat,

He smacks her if he doesn't get the reply he's after; she just turns the other cheek.

Creatures of Habit

What attracts a woman to certain types of men when she knows that he's so bad it,

Must be the fact that she can't help herself—merely, victim to instinct, regular creature of habit.

Propelled to find the flawed, it is no coincidence that she is not seeing,

The things that may bring her harm, she's compelled to what is worst for her being.

She seems to enjoy the heartache, revels in the hurt,

But it is her force of habit that keeps her circling the world of love in reverse.

If she, continuously, puts up with hitting, broken promises, and constantly quitting,

It may not be she finds the wrong men, instead, contentment with getting what she is getting.

Maybe, subconsciously, these are the things that excite her—the things that get her hot,

Explanation for her doing what she's always done and, continually, getting what she's always got.

Why else would she keep pushing and, relentlessly, keep on forging,

Forward with men that don't appreciate her worth and, to her efforts, are so abhorring?

Entering into the same setup and, somehow, expecting a new result,

Is, by definition, insanity and, to common sense, the strongest form of insult.

So before we pity the plight of this woman, dogging the men, calling them cads and hoes,

Understand, it may be what she craves—all results of the things that she chose.

Heavy-Handed

He walks in the house and drops his books; you could call it force of habit,

Too tired for much of anything else, just arriving home from football practice.

Soft sobs can be heard but, from where, he cannot see,

The sound's accented by a male's voice, slurring words with drunken speech.

He turns the kitchen corner, sees his mother, and decides to let her,

Tell him what is the matter, so he can deal with what has upset her.

He looks to his mother's lovely face and sees a trail of tears,

Eyes that are usually shimmering are, now, filled with hurt and fear.

He realizes there is be no possible way to keep her,

From crying—his father has gotten drunk, again, and beat her.

His mother always does her best to try to make the conscientious choice,

To hide her pain but, now, is betrayed by her trembling voice.

Daddy's gambled and drank his check away—blames Mama for him being broke,

After abusing her and waking from his slumber, he finds a cool blade up to his throat.

The son has grown disdain and disgust, watching his mother live life, in fear,

And declares if his father hits her, again, he will slit his throat from ear to ear.

No Play Thing

He says you're worthless, though, and makes you know with the dreams he sells you,

I say that you are priceless by what I know and the things I tell you.

You should consider giving time to a man that does adore you,

Instead of one that calls you "bitch" and "ho," like they are his pet names for you.

He sexes you to get rocks off, but could care less if you ever orgasm,

Rather than make love to you tenderly and enhance it through his passion.

Why should you accept all of his nothingness; he handles the rest, then, gets to you,

As if he's doing you a favor, like he's the best that you can do.

You hold him down in the toughest times; he's disrespectful, but you take it in stride,

After all that you do for him, he just treats you like a chick on the side.

Wake up, baby girl; don't let him walk over you and offend you,

When folks can do better—and, frankly, you can—they, more often than not, tend to.

A Sick Man Called "Ric"

It seems he is an alright guy; he talks like he is a real cool cat,

But underneath his cool demeanor, his beating heart is truly black.

He plays the role of a provider and acts like he's the perfect father,

But waits 'til his wife is off to work, so he can molest and rape his daughters.

You'd think by the way that he works out, he's trying to impress all the women,

It's really to feel like the man to his daughters, while they're crying when he is in them.

Discovery of his secret turned the town upside down—had everyone awed and vexed,

And his only explanation was that he was preparing his children for sex.

We can only imagine that he'd have a joint and a few drinks of liquor,

Then, call his daughter of choice to the room and proceed to have his way with her.

What a shame the effect he had on the girls and the impact he had on his wife,

Saying if they ever chose to tell anyone, in their sleep, he'd come and take their lives.

Crimes like these are a terrible thing; they make it so hard for the victims to give,

Their trust to other males in their world—it makes it impossible for them to truly live.

Though this is a fictitious account rooted in facts, about a man that I once knew,

This type of thing is happening, everyday; the culprits need to be brought to justice, too.

Ex Press

The ashes hit his tear-soaked shirt, as he blows smoke into the air,

His eyes are blurred from the fifth he's drank, pulling flames to the butt of his square.

His mind wonders to a time he'd, freely, given his girlfriend beatings,

While looking at damage he's done to her car; insecurity had told him she was cheating.

His body takes on a numbness, like it would if he were frost bit,

Thinking how he had a good thing, all along and, like a fool, he had lost it.

She'd put up with his abuse and tried to lift him when he was low,

He'd claimed that she did not love him, so she went out of her way to show.

So, currently, he waits outside her home like a stick-up kid might do,

Calculating his next move based on hers; he knows she has started night school.

Emotion clouds his judgment; he approaches as he sees her walking,

He made up his mind, long ago, so there is no need for any small talking.

This is the way, he reasons, that they can, now, be one,

So he shoots her twice in the belly, killing Lisa and their unborn son.

Desperation made him do it; he knows, now, he has no options left,

Once he murders her in cold blood, he turns the gun on himself.

Lisa has been forced to die, after years of being made to hurt,

Victim to senseless violence after repeated attempts to try and make it work.

This story is fictitious; I wish the ending could have been rearranged,

Please don't end up like little Lisa, thinking your abuser will ever change.

The love that we should

Apologizing for Womanizing

This world tells us to pursue the beauty queens that could grace covers of magazines,

But we should, still, consider the average girls and the ones that have low self-esteem.

No armed robberies like stickup kids; unlike the wise guys, there was no whacking,

Nevertheless, I have made some decisions that may have been just as impacting.

I won't play the role of saint; I, too, have done my share of dirt,

But I'm older, now, and have regrets on how I was foolish and caused you hurt.

In you, I saw things like low self-esteem; instead of helping you build it up and avoid it,

I did what I could to crack the code—to succeed in trying to exploit it.

Sometime, I was sincere; it wasn't just the usual lip service,

Others, though, it was to get a glimpse of your hips and your lip service.

You never were priority, though I made you feel so special,

My number one concern was to twist and turn you like a human pretzel.

Imagine how I felt, knowing you were catching feelings,

No matter how you kept concealing, I indulged, because your affection had no ceiling.

You gave what I took; I took all you had with no reciprocating return,

I taught you grown folks stuff; now, I'm the one with the lesson learned.

Good girl, I had but, bad girl, I might've turned you,

By me being so negligent with the issues that concerned you.

I had you at my disposal and used you like a tool,

And I ask that you forgive me for being such a fool.

I wasn't interested in your dreams—could care less if you were a visionary,

As long as I could get to the prize and get you in the missionary.

I made you think you controlled your life and that you really loved it,

You were good enough to roll and lay with, just not to be with out in public.

You made it known you had interest in dating; I said that I didn't care to,

But succeeded in convincing you that it was natural for me to "share" you.

I never paid attention; there was no feeling of guilt,

I was oblivious to the fact that I was wallowing in filth.

Getting laid from escapades was a pleasure cruise; I thought it as all games and fun when,

I realized each time I multiplied my number, I divided myself among them.

It wasn't 'til recently, I opened my eyes and, really, began to see,

That with each piece I got from you ladies, I got in exchange for a piece of me.

Don't think I don't feel the pain—all the heartache and the strife,

Knowing that I played so many games and will have guilt for the rest of my life.

This is definitely a new scene, beyond my previous smoke screens,

I've decided to try a new way, and delve into some new things.

I want to take the time to build and to show you a kinder,

Love to show yourself—a new respect for what's inside instead of behind you.

To that girl, you know who you are; you gave your heart and were willing to follow me,

I will never be able to make it right, but I do want to extend an apology.

For Sale by Owner

She said she had her love for sale; I told her I had an interest in trying,

She said that there'd be no test driving, if I didn't have an interest in buying.

I walked up to the lady, and said I only need a dab,

She asked if I'd be paying, now, or should she put it on my tab.

I assured that I liked to pay my debts—had no use for cash or debit,

And since I was upfront with payment, there'd be no need to extend a credit.

Too many had come and gone, she said; they could not respect the price,

Thought they knew what she expected, but they just could not get it right.

I scoffed and said what a shame, some people think so blandly and worthless,

Some things may have a value, but may be one that money cannot purchase.

She said that it seemed that I understood; this story had a part that I failed to mention,

The woman had her love for sale, sure, but only wanted to be paid attention.

Dusted Off

I see the pain in your eyes, even if you will not say,

It seems as though you bear a cross, and it will not go away.

Maybe you missed your father's embrace, so you're in need of a man,

Looking for right in the wrong places, receiving perceived love from wherever you can.

Perhaps, you weren't told that you were pretty—a diamond needing it's time to shine,

Putting physicality first instead of, simply, showing off your mind.

But, to you, I say, my sister, be strong and hold your head,

Don't be deterred by the road that decisions, in your past, might have led.

To you acting out in impulse, in your search to fill your needs,

Know that the present is a gift, and future is what you choose to be.

Because the thing about a gem and, more specifically, about a diamond,

Is when it's dusted off, no one can keep it from truly shining.

Carolina Leslie

There was this girl named Leslie; she was from the Carolinas,

And there's something about her that makes Leslie such a fine one.

She had four-quarter beauty—her fineness defined her,

Though she had an angelic face, she carried the devil behind her.

I wished upon a star with high hopes that I would find her,

And most subtle scents of her smell, served as the sweetest reminders.

I'd seen her the other day, as I walked through the mall,

We'd spoken and exchanged numbers, and so I decided to call.

Answering the phone, she had a soft, gentle voice,

Leslie could have who she wanted; I'm just glad I was her choice.

After all of the small talk, she let me into her past,

How men that she had dealt with all just seemed to want some ass.

Explaining it caught my attention, I could not even front,

Though not my number one concern, she had one hell of a rump.

Since I had been honest, she told me she admired that,

With a hint of a giggle, she said it was from her years of running track.

We really hit it off; it seems that listening is power,

Getting to know one another, well, it seems we laughed and joked for hours.

I asked if she'd like to get ice cream; she said she would rather be mine,

She said she'd become, to me, turned on, 'cause I didn't mention sex a single time.

The Thrill that Her Smile Gave

There was this girl that did appeal to me, small things let her reveal to me,

That, though, she had no need to be, she was plagued with insecurities.

I really couldn't pass this up—let this opportunity pass me by,

Make conversation with this girl, softly speak, and look into her eyes.

I asked if I could have her name; she, quickly, did oblige,

She said her name was Princess, and I told her that I could so see why.

She said she'd never liked it; children could be so ridiculing,

I assured her it was fitting; her Mama must have known what she was doing.

She told me it was flattering and thanked me for my kindness,

My response was that, to not notice, would hint to poor taste or a kind of blindness.

She grinned and said I that was too much; her cheeks began to redden,

The pleasure was all mine—just seeing an angelic face truly fit for Heaven.

The way her eyes shine and slim; dimples draw back from her chin,

A smile so pretty, free, and full, I told jokes to see her smile, again.

Because I was preoccupied by the thrill that her smile gave,

We laughed and joked and shot the breeze for the whole rest of the day.

Unparalleled Pieces

Smiles must be works of dream weavers; lips form curvatures that astound all around them,

Tickled to death from simple delights, eyes dance to the music of life that surrounds them.

Conversations reveal the cutest curiosity and, yet, a mature understanding of the world,

Evidence of class and sophistication all within the shell of a country girl.

I will not try to lie; I'd be remiss to not acknowledge physique,

But, for me, the essence of your beauty is the aura of your persona's mystique.

Your body may prove to be a feast, unparalleled pieces of eye candy,

But my sweet tooth, for you, will likely be, for the treats my eyes cannot see.

Eyes Never Lie

They tell a telling story, for a while, paralyze,

Through your radiant beauty, what stand out are your eyes.

Skin so smooth and so silky—complexion, somewhat, exotic,

Moving grace like pendulum, I find them so hypnotic.

Chocolate brown orbs are enticing—could drive the preacher man wild,

I feel like you're doing magic each time they're enhanced by your smile.

Seeing you is amazing; watching you could content me enough,

You put me in a daze when your pretty eyes brighten up.

Works of art, they are—more than tools you use to see,

To the world, a disservice, each time you close them for sleep.

As long as your eyes view the world, beauty has a place to stay,

And true beauty is seen, each time you awake to face the day.

Daydream Date

Her eyes glistened like lights, at night; they were enchanting and exciting,

When she smiled, the form that graced her face was so warm and inviting.

Her presence was so regal—her skin as smooth as silk,

The way her hair hugged her high cheek bones, in the present, was a gift.

With such a natural beauty, she could bring strong men to their knees,

Though I loved the way she walked away, it hurt my heart to see her leave.

She was modest about her looks; with conceit, she was discreet,

She was a marvel in appearance, but a beast when she began to speak.

To a woman who seemed to be hand-carved, what would be a proper compliment to give her?

Saying she is a true gift from God is the only description that befits her.

Now that I'm awake from my daydream, let me recompose my demeanor,

Maybe I'll never have her, in life, but I'm blessed that, at least, I have seen her.

I Imagine

I imagine your hair is still organized in chaos, like tossed with salad utensils,

With lips so pursed and plump—perfect like outlined with a pencil.

I imagine your silhouette is a perfect outline; even imperfections don't give you flaw lines,

From the curve of your nose to the chisel of your cheeks and jaw line.

I imagine you bite your lip a bit when interest is piqued—your eyes squint if something's funny,

I imagine your scent to be like rose petals, and your taste like the sweetest of honeys.

Strong you are with a will of steel; independence is a muscle to you, and you flex it,

I imagine when you are allowed to feel vulnerable but safe, that you find it even more sexy.

I Like You, Do You Like Me?

I have seen you, on occasion,

Left me in utter dismay.

Your grace seemed so amazin,'

Beauty took my breath, away.

Each time I've seen you, I've frozen,

My shy tongue won't let me say it.

Maybe lame, but I've chosen,

To let my pen and paper convey it.

I hope you do not mind, how I have chosen to approach it,

Or think that I am running game.

Of your class and beauty, I have taken notice,

With only hopes of learning your name.

I cannot believe I am too shy to talk,

Passing letters like the number one fan.

Having a crush like a young school boy,

When, in reality, I am a grown ass man.

I feel a lot better—got that all off my chest,

You are cute, and I'm attracted is all.

I don't know how you will feel, next,

But here's my number to call.

Last Did

There's a chance I could be a playboy—possibility that I am a hoodlum,

But, then again, it is possible that I might actually prove to be a good one.

When I say that you are pretty, it could be game to get in your pants,

Or I could just want to know your name and, maybe, a chance to dance.

Giving me too much too soon, could set you up for me to sex you,

Or letting me learn about you might give me a chance to respect you.

Serenity says maybe I'm out to hurt you; courage lets you decide whether to make that true,

My question, now, to you is, do you know the difference between the two?

Do you know how to pick a good one? Truth is, you probably don't,

But if you want to find love but are afraid, chances are, that you probably won't.

Caution is always a wise approach, but don't be crippled by what the past did,

How can you ever receive love that today's man gives, always reliving what the last did?

Baby Girl

Oh, how I want your hand to hold,

You have snatched my heart and touched my soul.

Since the first time I look into your eyes,

I knew you were special—angel in disguise.

I feel like I want to scream or to shout it out loud,

Because I can't have you with me, right here and right now.

Deep in my heart, I know it's my pleasure and, too, my duty,

To whisper sweet nothings in your ear while feelin' on your booty.

I want all of your love, free-willing, not demanded,

And I want your kisses so bad, I can hardly stand it.

If you rejected heartfelt attempts, my heart would be damaged,

On a mission, I'm searching for something and I can't leave empty-handed.

You are the cream of the crop—the cock of the walk—most pretty of reflections,

If you were mine, you would find, you'd be showered, drunk, with my affection.

You give feelings down my spine like pleasant surprises when you are startled,

I could love you even more than an alcoholic does his bottle.

There is nothing that I can do, like a fifteen with no hit,

Barren like a window with no shutter.

Addicted like nicotine in a cigarette,

There is only you and could be no other.

So many to thank for making you—a thanks so long overdue,

I will thank God, every night, when I pray, for giving me the only you.

Do not hesitate to put me in line, if it seems you don't center my world,

I couldn't do that if I wanted to, because you are my baby—my baby girl.

Forbidden Fruit

Let me see your face light up like lights,

Let me make your cheek bones rise.

Let me excite, in you, your heart's greatest delight,

Let me get lost as I stare into your eyes.

Your body's perfectly fit in my arms,

And your lips, they taste so sweet.

The truth is I don't think I can feel harm,

Anytime that you are close to me.

I know that there are some times,

When things don't go like we think they should.

But even with keeping this in mind,

In my mind, I still feel good.

'Cause, though it seems like I can't have you,

And our future together is grim.

I know you feel the same that I do,

And you want me rather than him.

Not everything is all bad news and sobs,

All is not just filled with bad habits.

I see that we can fight like cats and dogs,

And come back and make love like rabbits.

I could not possibly say what I wanted,

I had to be discreet in a sort.

The length of this expression is stunted,

I could keep going but must cut it short.

Ivory

I've missed you in my dream land, my quaint and comfy confines,

For I have grown so accustomed, to our regular meeting of minds.

Though I knew I would never have you, I cannot begin to front,

Don't misinterpret my last statement, as a discount to my wants.

From the moment that I first saw you, when I spoke and you came to see,

Pretty brown eyes seemed to mesmerize my mind, and you smiled so gingerly.

The perfect shape, the perfect weight,

And one visit demonstrated the perfect date.

Honeysuckle Sweetness

Focused kisses of caramel, her smile could provoke prophets,

Every time I see her smile, I have insatiable cravings for chocolate.

All in all, she's my menthol; she always lifts and soothes me,

Like crackling thunder following lightning, she knows just how to move me.

Subtle and genteel, precious each time she calls my name,

Like a leaf in a puddle—a mist in the midst of pounding rain.

Her attitude is never rude; she is not pushy or violent,

Compassion is, plainly, in her eyes; emotion rips through her silence.

And I never thought that I'd feel the things that I have felt,

The way this girl amazed me, I thought she would make me melt.

Not pushing up on you, don't misunderstand; I know that is not you and me,

Just had some free time and thought you should know, to me, what you have come to be.

Neanderthal Drawl

This is a call to action—an attack on being tacky,

An assault on talking raunchy—the words that set the world aback, see.

Sayings and expressions that help to build the future's tomb,

Strangling our daughters' strength before they even exit the womb.

It's directed at women, but a detriment to all,

The controversy in question, we'll call Neanderthal Drawl.

It, slowly, inflicts pain, when we choose to repress respect,

Like a stinging splinter in a finger or thorns ripping into flesh.

Society may see it as nothing, but just know it hurts them so,

Each and every time you choose, to call a woman a "bitch" or "ho."

Direct or indirect, it's all the same; it doesn't matter the direction,

Whether blatant or passive entertaining of self-depreciating indiscretions.

Not comprehending what I'm mentioning, it is simple as this,

You might not call her out of her name, just buy drinks and encourage her to strip.

No one is ever perfect, but just let me assure you,

We have to change this habit, if we aim to preserve our future.

Plain and Simple Love

If you're promised a 'real nigga,' it's probably how it sounds—such ignorance is bliss,

Love and dedication is all I have to give, so 'real nigga shit,' I'm just not it.

But, maybe, that is what you need—a man that wants to treat you right,

That, genuinely, wants to show and try and give you the finer things in life.

Now, anyone can take you out to eat, dancing, or to catch a movie,

But if that exists with the lack of love, what is it really proving?

I could manipulate you with such devices—promise to lasso the moon out of the sky,

But, then, I'd be doing the same thing—using the same tricks as the other guy.

See, cats will tell you anything; many will do whatever to attempt to win,

The bait has to be tasty for you to take the hook, in order to reel you in.

So, though, you could go for the show—the glitz of shiny things and dreams,

I hope that you see my heart's desire—treating you like a queen with simple things.

Wants and Needs

I want you more than words can say—more than I have wanted anything,

I need you like a baby needs a bottle—like a dry cleaner needs his steam.

I want you with an urge so strong that passion would override my strength,

Like a fool with royal guidance, I need your mind to help me make sense.

I want to see your lips pucker when you pout, your hair tucked behind your ear,

I need to feel the warmth of your body and gentle breaths, each time that you are near.

I want your scent to fill my nostrils—to know that my touch makes you shutter,

I need you to become another half to me—a bond I have had with no other.

I want your hands to rub my head, reassuring me that I can win,

Caressing and encouraging—I need to feel like a little kid, again.

I want your eyes to shift from mine to my lips, all because you want to kiss me,

I need you to count down the time until you see me, just because you miss me.

I want to be soft enough to hold you, but hard enough to handle you,

I need you to trust me, unconditionally, and know I would not scandal you.

I want to be the man of your dreams—your knight with full armor that shines,

I need to have a position in some of your thoughts; you have a place in all of mine.

Fragrance of the Peel

Searching high and low, and digging even deeper,

Doing all I can and hoping that I can reach you.

Let it marinate a second, and tell me how I should cook that,

Wanting you so much, I almost taste it, but don't know where to look at.

(It's true)

Unveil your beauty, let your presence be known, step from behind the cloud,

Then, maybe, I can sleep at night, 'cause my heart won't cry so loud.

The most beautiful things are so seldom seen—their sunlight shaded by the trees,

Money buys diamonds that don't always shine, but the best things, in life, come free.

I'm amused with the sensual ambience—sexuality that you keep,

And the sheer do of your parlay view is unparalleled; no one else competes.

Just like the mist of a waterfall or a single rain drop,

Gathering constant grace in its steady descent to bottom from top.

(Precisely)

You bring honesty and truth, to the words out of my mouth,

And you are one of the great ones just like Sonny told C. about.

Like the succulence of ripe fruit or the fragrance of the peel,

Or a cool sweeping breeze in new springtime dandelion fields.

You are Rembrandt and Picasso, Michelangelo, too,

The Mona Lisa is cute, but has nothing on you.

You are equivalent to a stallion; it would be an honor to shoe you,

So there is no wonder that many-a-man would try to boo you.

The Wonder of the Woman

What makes up a woman; what adds to her wonder,

What about her makes the world stand still—commands respect like rumbling thunder?

The next regularly scheduled visit can never seem to come too soon,

All eyes raise and heads turn, whenever she walks into a room.

A lady, knowing how to handle herself, when the nosy public may surround,

And, too, having unshakable faith, when trouble is abound.

Precious as a flower, too strong to take the path of least resistance,

She bears the burden of this troubled world, responsible for all of our existence.

What is it about this woman which makes her worth such recognition?

Is it her all-natural beauty or her right-on intuition?

God's most treasured gifts to the world—not just to the lucky man,

So I say, with pride, to you, it is a marvel to welcome to the Wonder of the Woman.

Probably Never Knew

The longing for your beauty is like a battle I have never won,

Enough to take me to new places—do new things I've never done.

My wishing and wanting you as my one and only, you can believe it's true,

And it may seem like I'm selling a dream, because you probably never knew.

You never knew I'd be your confidant—hold secrets you've always kept,

Content just to hold you, gently, caressing your ears and scalp while you slept.

There's no way you could guess, I never want you lonely when you're alone,

Or that I wanted to shelter you from pain or give you a home to call your own.

You never knew your past haunts me, too, because I can't stand in your place to face it,

And there's nothing I can do to take it back—there is no chance I could erase it.

You never knew your vote of confidence makes me aim to be the very best,

Or that I would rather have your eyes' tenderness than the firmness of your breasts.

Willingness, Readiness

Far more than a beauty, but nothing less than a queen,

You are a snapshot of excellence, refined mold of esteem.

From the top of your head to the edge of your toenails,

There's a masterpiece in the making, and what a story it can tell.

When my eyes find you, they find pretty plus class,

Much more to you than just a booty; I'm not attracted to just your ass.

That's not what caught my eye—at least, not all, you know?

You have an aura about yourself—magnificent shine, a glow.

It says you are more than nothingness, pettiness,

But, instead, there is, with you, willingness and a readiness.

To Serve and Protect

I want to kiss your sleeping eyelids, hold you during the storm,

Protect you through the midnight hour just to serve you breakfast in the morning.

You're the only one my bones Jones for; no other girl could ever best you,

I'll cook and clean the kitchen, tonight, because I know you need your rest, too.

I yearn to kiss you and explore you, finding each and every spot,

Love you and show you that I need you—then, please you until you beg me to stop.

No treatment like you're second class or feeling like you should 'know your role,'

Whatever makes you smile, I'm satisfied; your overall happiness is my goal.

I'll take my time to wine and dine you; just, you, be patient, and I will find you,

And if you ever feel like I lag behind, I'll give more love and kindness to remind you.

Rub your shoulders to ease your tension or slowly caress your spine,

Any need you have I'll find and fill, trying to drive you out of your mind.

Majestic Yet Domestic

So incredible and free, what a great day that you have made this,

Majestic, yet domestic—no hair weaves, makeup, or fakeness.

Innocent, yet mysterious, I cannot fathom exactly what is this,

I watch until my eyes are dry; I don't blink, because I don't want to miss this.

Your smile is so pleasant like a cool autumn breeze,

When your hair sways and moves, like blowing leaves in the trees.

Your presence is evident; it seems able to pause the time,

How delighted I am, taking freeze frame after frame with my mind.

Of you standing there, twinkling the skies with your eyes,

Something magical about you seems to make the butterflies fly.

A garden of blooming lilacs would be such an astonishing scene,

But could not hold a candle to the beauty of you that is so supreme.

Natural Beauty in Abundance

A beauty so mythical, best minds of our time could not understand it,

Figure like a talented hand, formed and sculpted her from granite.

Rich complexion is so aptly fit, skin resembles the smoothest cream,

Jumps out to embrace the world, while it shines through self-esteem.

There is no denying the fact of this girl's lovely face,

Punctuate it with the fact she's as thick as Salisbury steak.

Exquisite beauty—front and profile views parallel that of the back,

Lips bloom like blossoms in the spring—eyes slant like peepers of Persian cats.

Her presence is felt and speaks through in volumes, although her mouth is often silent,

Beauty is out of reality's norm—exotic as though she were from the islands.

Aura of a deity, everlasting fragrance of a flower,

Time, with her, serves as a cherished treasure; jewels become outweighed by hours.

Eyes always probe and stare—lips, so sweet, when they pucker and pout,

Beautiful thoughts on a beautiful mind, and I long to figure them out.

Natural beauty in abundance, like straight from the hands of the Creator,

Pecan-colored hue, so true, to the privileges that rest in reserve within Mother Nature.

Nubian Queen

She's got skin like brown sugar, and her eyes are chocolate brown,

With a figure-eight frame, her hips are nice and round.

She can stop the world with a finger and can light it up with her smile,

Her eyes possess happiness and strength that flood just like the Nile.

Her smile is a definite sight that all of Mankind should see,

More spectacular than July 4th, she could charge an admission fee.

The turbulence, the storm, negativity and hurt—she has been through it all,

She's been bound with chains and hurt and pain, but still rises and refuses to fall.

Clout? She has it—she holds the rank; well known, she has a lot of pull,

Able to be a natural wonder of the world, she is just too wonderful.

Forget what you have heard; she's the best there is, will be, or ever has been,

The most beautiful person God could create, she is the Nubian Queen.

Two Parts

She is clearly rather than probably a blessing in biology—a very special specimen,

Too constant to be a variable in the equation—much more than ever lesser than.

Her compassion's that of missionary—an eye that glares like that of a tiger,

Integrity is never a second thought; you are cussing if you ever call her a liar.

Whether in calamity and chaos or solace and serenity, she stays the same,

The world doesn't understand, when it sees her inner peace—just how her joy remains.

Ever-ready to hand out mercy, she never allows malice and hatred to linger,

In times of glory, she wants the backseat; in times of blame, she points no fingers.

(I trust…)

She is really and truly something, like Shug Avery singing to Miss Celie,

Never over-the-top and extra, but filled to the rim with emotion and feelings.

And any person—woman or man—that is fool enough to doubt her,

Could have never ever encountered her and must know nothing about her.

Love Her Not Fight Her

Because, in a word, she is a BEAST—so reserved and, yet, so free,

Determined to see her family eat, but not mere scraps; she aims to feast.

Nowhere near a square, by far, she understands the adage of all work and no play,

It is trite to say "she has a Super Woman cape in the closet," but I will say it, anyway.

(Believe...)

Strength is one of her strongest strong points; she is one hell of a lady,

Agile enough to juggle groceries on one hip and, on the other, a crying baby.

Confident enough to rise and shine—able to speak next to anybody,

Worldly enough to be able to be a social butterfly at any gathering or party.

Sought out for advice, there's weight in whatever she chooses to say,

She doesn't just recite words from the Word; she strives to live them, every day.

Seemingly defying the laws of physics, her beauty says not that she is aging,

Rather, her DNA proves to the world, she is part incredible and part amazing.

Love Her Not Fight Her

Good steward of what she's been entrusted; she's a glorification of her maker,

The twirling world tosses but cannot shake her; likes of man don't make or break her.

Even in the darkest, coldest winter, she radiates such light and warmth,

Though she cannot stop the rain, her very voice seems to calm the storm.

Just a subtle smile from her is a sign of reassuring reliance,

Her touch can either soothe the soul or it can succeed in inciting a riot.

She shows you that she knows how, from the schoolhouse to the church house,

She needs no proof like a book, in order to back up the knowledge from her mouth.

(It's clear…)

She always aces with flying colors, no matter how life chooses to test her,

Her instincts leave her prepared for the weather, regardless of how you dress her.

In spite of her personal hurdles, she is never too selfish to try and nurture,

Willingness to give the rest the best and save for self what's left is evidence of virtue.

She is cleansing like a flowing stream—nourishing like the ground,

Rooted and strong like an old oak tree, giving covering protection like a cloud.

An essential to building, like dampened mortar to brick,

Purifying and illuminating, like the flame closest to the wick.

(Please know…)

Her heritage is present, when her hips flow from her sides and back,

And her eyes, they tell a story, that her lips cannot begin to match.

It's not that she is so compelled or needs to feel that she is teaching lessons,

But her life is its own lesson plan—a natural teacher, and she just can't help it.

Never the worst, by far, but she doesn't claim to be close to perfect,

No man alive, dead, or not yet born, could try to deny what her worth is.

The bean from which our blossoms bud—to her existence there, clearly, is no rival,

Her triumphant story should be our priority; we should forever love her—never fight her.

www.ingramcontent.com/pod-product-compliance
Lightning Source LLC
Chambersburg PA
CBHW071840020426
42331CB00007B/1797